ENDORSEMENTS

"Every woman should read Dyed in the Wool as it provides a different perspective of the action women need to carve our society into a better place. I identified with Hadassah, commonly known as Esther who was a fearless activist reshaping the world for those who do not have the power to do so themselves."

– *Ida Byrd-Hill*, President,
Uplift Inc.

"This is a Great Book! My wife is so knowledgeable of the Word of God and she brings out powerful truths through twelve short stories. People who may not read the bible will be inspired to do so because of this book."

– *Clinton L. Tarver*, Proud Husband

"Linda Lee has done an incredible job researching and discerning such beauty in the history of these women. These stories are gems which provide us insight and revelation in a time where women are in need of affirmation the most!"

– *Jessica Ann Tyson*, President,
Frederick Douglass Foundation of Michigan

Dr. Linda Lee Tarver, "through her extensive research and tremendous knowledge of the scriptures, provide Republican women with the greatest in kingdom tools and biblical lessons that will inspire, educate and provoke a courageous stand."

*– **Dr. Thurston Willoughby**, President, Kingdom University International, AICSC*

"I met Linda Lee more than 20 years ago at a Michigan State GOP convention in Lansing, Michigan. Although new to politics, Linda Lee was very eager to learn. At the time, not many African-American women were actively engaged in politics, so she and I were immediately drawn to each other. Linda Lee identifies politics as her favorite sport or hobby. Politics has become her passion and why she has honed her craft and excelled in her political prowess. Lauded for her political skill and charm, Linda Lee has earned her place among the great Republican women in Michigan.

Ten years after we met, Linda Lee and I started the Alliance of Black Republicans (ABR) - an organization essential to attracting and retaining non-traditional Republicans, predominately minorities. The ABR set about educating others, using our nations' founding documents and Constitution, the Grand Ol' Party's history along with its tenets and platform to affirm that the Party of Lincoln is strong and inclusive of all.

Linda Lee comes highly credentialed, having earned a bachelor's degree in business management and a master's degree in Organizational Psychology. Now working toward a second doctorate degree through Grand Canyon University in Education, but with great humility, she refers to herself as a 'Sunday school teacher' who has been catapulted to a large classroom called America. Her wit and determination commands respect and credibility.

Dr. Tarver's political passion is surpassed only by her love of God and His people. An avid student of the word of God, Linda Lee Tarver's tenacity culminated in completing her Doctorate in Theology degree from Kingdom University International. This accomplishment prompted her to share the message contained in the pages of this magnificent book.

"Dyed in the Wool," guides the reader through twelve intricate and powerful lives of women in the Word of God. The title may appear odd at first, leaving the reader to ponder how it relates to the women or to the Word of God. Dr. Tarver uses the phrase, 'dyed in the wool' - as coined so poignantly by Abolitionist Frederick Douglass in describing his own political party devotion - to describe the commitment of the women she highlights. Metaphorically speaking, 'dyed in the wool' perfectly describes the indelible, permanence that their commitment made to the 'fabric' of their lives. Just as Frederick Douglass shared that he was fully and irrevocably part of the fabric of his Party, Linda Lee Tarver likewise seeks to engage Republican women to become irrevocably committed to God."

*— **Kim M. Porter-Hoppe**, President, MI Republican Women's Club (Virtual Club), Former Presidential Appointee under President George W. Bush, Former Member of the Committee of African-American Republican Leadership (C.A.R.L.), Former Member of the Michigan Black Republicans (M.B.R.), Former President of the Alliance of Black Republicans (A.B.R.)*

Dyed in the Wool:
A Biblical Guide for Republican Women

DYED
in the WOOL

DR. LINDA LEE TARVER
FOREWORD BY EVANGELIST ALVEDA C. KING

LIBERTY HILL PUBLISHING

Liberty Hill Publishing
2301 Lucien Way #415
Maitland, FL 32751
407.339.4217
www.libertyhillpublishing.com

Unless otherwise indicated, Scripture quotations taken from
the Holy Bible, New International Version (NIV). Copyright
© 1973, 1978, 1984, 2011 by Biblica, Inc.™. Used by
permission. All rights reserved.

Printed in the United States of America.

ISBN-13: 978-1-54563-967-2

DEDICATION

This book is dedicated to my wonderful husband, Clinton Tarver, my precious children Jennifer Lee-Williams, and Terrance Williams, and the man entrusted with my soul, my spiritual father Pastor/Teacher Dr. H. Levi McClendon, III.

TABLE OF CONTENTS

ACKNOWLEDGEMENTS

This book would not have been possible without the prayers, support, and encouragement of my Pastor H. Levi McClendon, III and First Lady Mya McClendon. God's continued blessing to a pastor to the pastorless and hopeless, Dr. Alveda King. Special acknowledgement to Pastor/Dr. Willie and Lady Angie Loggins, Dr. Thurston and Dr. Deborah Willougby, Bishop/Dr. Ira Combs Jr., my Mt. Zion All Nations Bible Church Family, my Republican mentor and brother, Norm Shinkle, and my sisters in the cause, Kim Hoppe, Sarina White, Dawn Dodge, Ann Schockett, Jessica Ann Tyson, Kelly Mitchell, Ida Byrd-Hill, Ronna Romney McDaniel, Ruth Johnson, and more.

This book is birth from my love of the Party of Lincoln and the people who are led by the Spirit of God to do a great work. As Republicans who love and trust the Lord, we have been asked, "And what does the Lord require of you? To act justly and to love mercy and to walk humbly with your God" (Micah 6:8). To the endless number of Republican leaders across the state of Michigan that encouraged me to stay the conservative course and become the activist the Lord Himself has graced me to be, I thank you.

Dyed in the Wool pays tribute to Frederick Douglass whose work as an abolitionist and Black Republican is celebrated today. To my fellow Black Republicans who are 'dyed in the wool,' thank you. To the beautiful women and sisters of the National Federation of Republican Women (NFRW), I am so blessed to be a part of this organization.

The most heartfelt acknowledgement is the women of the Republican Women's Federation of Michigan (RWFM). It has been my deepest honor to be elected to lead you and one that I will forever be grateful for.

ABOUT DR. ALVEDA KING

*E*vangelist Alveda C. King works toward her purpose in life, to glorify God.

She currently serves as a Pastoral Associate and Director of Civil Rights for the Unborn, the African-American Outreach for Priests for Life and Gospel of Life Ministries. She is also a voice for the Silent No More Awareness Campaign, sharing her testimony of two abortions, God's forgiveness, and healing. In 2018, Dr. Alveda King was appointed by President Trump to the Frederick Douglass Bicentennial Commission.

The daughter of the late civil rights activist Rev. A.D. King and his wife Naomi Barber King, Alveda grew up in the civil rights movement led by her uncle, Dr. Martin Luther King, Jr. Her family home in Birmingham, Alabama, was bombed, as was her father's church office in Louisville, Kentucky. Alveda was jailed during the open housing movement. She sees the prolife movement as a continuation of the civil rights struggle.

Evangelist King is a former college professor and served in the Georgia State House of Representatives. She is a recipient of the Life Prize Award (2011), the Cardinal John O'Connor Pro-Life Hall of Fame Award (2011) from the Legatus organization and the Civil Rights Award from Congress of Racial Equality (CORE) (2011). She is a best-selling author; among her books are *King Rules: Ten Truths for You, Your Family, and Our Nation to Prosper, How Can the Dream Survive if we Murder the Children?* and *I Don't Want Your Man, I Want My Own*. She is an accomplished actress and songwriter. The Founder of Alveda King Ministries, Alveda is also the recipient of an honorary Doctorate of Laws degree from Saint Anselm College. She has served on several boards, including Heartbeat International, Georgia Right to Life, MLK Center, Bible Curriculum in Public Schools and Abortion Recovery International (ARIN). She is also a member of the National Black Prolife Coalition (NBPC) and is a Senior Fellow with the Howard Center for Family, Religion & Society. Alveda is a regular columnist for Newsmax.com "Insiders" section and a Fox News contributor. Evangelist King lives in Atlanta, where she is the grateful mother of six and a doting grandmother.

FOREWORD
By Evangelist Alveda C. King

We no longer need to wonder where Dr. Linda Lee Tarver gains her inspiration and strength to accomplish remarkable feats and exploits. We also can understand how she charts her course through the some-times-choppy waters of life's ups and downs. We must finally be mindful that while Dr. Linda is a bright light in the contemporary political arena, her worth and values extend far beyond the political realm.

Case in point: Dr. Tarver has taken time to design and pen down an intriguing treatise which is also a roadmap to suc-cess in today's political climate. While the book is written primarily with a female republican audience in mind, many of the principles herein can be appreciated by women and men who want to further understand the roles of godly women in today's challenging times.

DYED IN THE WOOL is a descriptive title which gives insight into the successes of godly women highlighted in the chapters and a deeper awareness of the mind and heart of our author as well. Dr. Tarver has taken a page from the lives of great women of God who have gone before her. Yet, Dr. Tarver is also a pioneer in that she is calling for an awakening of women in the twenty-first century.

By it's very definition, DYED IN THE WOOL reveals a steadfastness of heart that is required to run the course of life in such a way as to accomplish mighty goals while establishing a pattern for those who will follow us. Each chapter in this book reveals and unlocks the secrets of how to use the examples of women of the Bible to attain our deepest and most heartfelt desires; to make a difference for increasing good in the world, to be beacons of light for generations to come.

In daring women to live godly lives, Dr. Tarver is throwing down a gauntlet before those who are challenged with indifference, compromise and middle of the road syndrome. DYED IN THE WOOL is not for the faint of heart. She challenges us to be "living epistles" in our roles as wives, mothers, breadwinners, public figures, ministers; no matter what our missions are, we must first be Christ centered.

Perhaps we expected just another political ex-parte; a one-dimensional one-sided dissertation. Dr. Tarver intrigues and inspires us with a bird's eye view into women who faced some of the same challenges we face here in the twenty-first century. As we delve into the lives and lessons learned from such Bible women as Zelophehad's five daughters, the Samaritan woman, Rahab the Harlot, The Nameless Prostitute, Judge Deborah, Jochebed, Hadessah, Lois and Eunice, Mary, Mother of Jesus, Joanna and Suzanna, Mary, Mother of John Mark, and Jephthah's Daughter, our minds will be renewed, and we will come away enriched with tools for living as successful and victorious Christian women. Be encouraged as you turn every page. God bless you.

~ Evangelist Alveda C. King

DYED IN THE WOOL

*M*y calling in life is to glorify God. Christians are charged to preach the Good News, and part of preaching is accomplished through teaching. Another tradition for the preacher is to become a living epistle, or an open letter. I am writing just such an open letter to you, as a teacher and a lifelong member of Mt. Zion All Nations Bible Church in DeWitt, MI.

Now that we have a starting point, I want to move directly into a discussion that will have meaning in the lives of everyone, that is, people in the political world that surrounds us. We are each on a political journey, even as we focus on our daily lives and families. For me, my political journey began with realizing that I am tired of being sick and tired. The Republican Party platform and principles align with my own standards more than do those of the Democrats, but how could I make my principles live in the political world? Scared at first, I looked for a meeting and a place to share and grow. I went from armchair, to county chair, to vice chair. As I have grown, I have found that my opinions, voice, and message now reach a broader audience.

My political journey allowed me to read about a great man named Frederick Douglass. He was an abolitionist and activist. Most remarkably, Mr. Douglass was a Republican. This book was inspired by his words, "I am a Republican, a black, dyed in the wool Republican, and I never intend to belong to any other party than the party of freedom and progress." I share his great sentiment and passion for my

Party, but I am fully committed to building the Kingdom of God. I desire to inspire others to become fully 'dyed in the wool' in the great works they have been called to do.

Proverbs 31:8 says, "Speak up for those who cannot speak for themselves, for the rights of all who are destitute." As a biblical teacher, I have selected some of the women of the Word who were great conservative political leaders and activists who have changed the world. Each woman had a unique contribution to the political landscape, and each speaks to us today as Republican women. In this book, I wanted to guide others along the path from being worried about our country to being active in building the Kingdom. As examples we can follow, I have selected twelve stories of women who inspire me as a mother, a Republican activist, a political leader, a community contributor, and most importantly, as a child of the living God.

I will now introduce the following women to bless you, encourage you, and inspire you. Each woman undertook a specific task that informs our lives today.

These women are (1) Zelophehad's five daughters, (2) the Samaritan woman, (3) Rahab, (4) The Nameless Prostitute, (5) Judge Deborah, (6) Jochebed, (7) Hadessah, (8) Lois and Eunice, (9) Mary, Mother of Jesus, (10) Joanna and Suzanna, (11) Mary, Mother of John Mark, and (12) Jephthah's Daughter. Each has accomplished a specific task, teaching us about God's plan for our lives. Each will be described in the chapters to follow.

Table 1

Women Who Glorified God

Title	Lesson Taught
Zelophehad's Daughters	Republican Women Are Great Litigators
Samaritan Woman	Republican Women Persuade the Masses
Rahab	Republican Women Recognize the People and Power of God
The Nameless Prostitute	Republican Women Choose Life
Judge Deborah	Republican Women Judge Wisely
Jochebed	Republican Women Build Arks for Their Children
Hadessah	Republican Women Are Prayerful, Fearless Activists
Lois and Eunice	Republican Women Share Their Faith
Mary, Mother of Jesus	Republican Women Are Effective Lobbyists
Joanna and Suzanna	Republican Women Are Generous Donors
Mary, Mother of John Mark	Republican Women Pray
Jephthah's Daughter	Republican Women Are Committed to the End

CHAPTER 1

ZELOPHEHAD'S DAUGHTERS: REPUBLICAN WOMEN ARE GREAT LITIGATORS

*T*he first of many wonderful women identified in this book are the five daughters of Zelophehad. Numbers 27 lists the names of the daughters as Mahlah, Noah, Hoglah, Milkah, and Tirzah. These women were part of the Manasseh clan, the son of Joseph. In Numbers 25, the Lord was displeased with the sexual immorality of men who had lain with Moabite women. Many men and women died in a plague that the Lord caused. In Numbers 26, the Lord told Moses to take the second census of the men so the land the Lord promised could be divided. This is the account of the women who successfully litigated their inheritance.

The discussion of the daughters of Zelophehad is but one example in the Word of God that demonstrates a powerful message of God's love for women—especially women who stand for what is right. Women in that day did not have rights to land. The legacy was passed down to the males in the family only. If there were no males, the father's name would immediately end. This was unfortunate for women who were mere chattel to men—but not to God.

Numbers 27:2 reports the five litigating sisters going to the tent of meeting and standing before Eleazar the priest, Moses, and the leaders of the whole assembly. They said, "Our father died in the wilderness. He was not among Korah's followers, who banded together against the Lord, but he died for his own sin and left no sons. Why should our father's name disappear from his clan because he had no son? Give us property among our father's relatives" (Num. 27:3-4). This was unheard of! However, Moses was compelled by their argument to bypass the leaders and take the issue to the Lord God Himself.

The Bible tells us that the Lord said to Moses, "What Zelophehad's daughters are saying is right. You must certainly give them property as an inheritance among their father's relatives and give their father's inheritance to them" (Num. 27:6-7). After God commanded this, case law for property rights was established in Israel, and from then on, women were afforded to inherit from their father. The Lord honored the sisters' petition, and Moses understood the argument must be heard by the ruling judge, which is God. The property law case was successfully litigated and taken on, and it became "the force of law for the Israelites, as the Lord commanded Moses" (Num. 27:11).

Republican women are good litigators who speak up where there is no precedence. Republican women challenge the status quo, look at right versus wrong, and do not assume that the Lord God represents a sexist culture. Republican women prepare a compelling case and argument based on the truth and rule of law. Like the five daughters of Zelophehad, Republican women are great litigators.

CHAPTER 2

SAMARITAN WOMAN: REPUBLICAN WOMEN PERSUADE THE MASSES

*T*he next powerful woman in the Word of God is the nameless Samaritan (Jn. 4:7). In that day, it was understood that the Jews and the Samaritans were not on good terms and did not associate with each other (Jn. 4:9). In fact, many Jews would travel well out of their way to avoid encounters with the Samaritans. Jesus did not. One day, Jesus was tired from His journey and settled at Jacob's well for a drink (Jn. 4:7). It was highly irregular for Jews to speak to Samaritans and unheard of for Jews to speak to women. During Jesus' encounter with the Samaritan woman, He told her that He knew she had been divorced four times and that the man she was currently living with was not her husband (Jn. 4:17-18).

The revelation about this woman's past—and the fact that a Jew would speak to her at all—caused her to take note and recognize that Jesus was a man of God. In the exchange, Jesus told her that He was the Messiah she was waiting for. Upon hearing this Good News, the four-time divorcee or widow who was shacking up with a man could not hold her peace. The Word of God says that the woman left her water jar—and her shame—to quickly go and tell the people the Good News of the Messiah. How awesome it must have been. The record of this encounter with the Samaritan woman is that "many of the Samaritans from that town believed in him because of the woman's testimony" (Jn. 4:39a).

The record of what occurred did not end with the Samaritan woman's testimony and excitement. She persuaded the townspeople to hear the man of God for themselves. Once they heard from Jesus, they believed on Him (Jn. 4:42). The petition and persuasion of the Samaritan woman changed an entire city. This remarkable event is evidence again of God's love for women and how He uses them to fulfill His divine plan and purpose.

Republican women are passionate persuaders of the Truth. Despite their backgrounds, failures, and flaws, Republican women who have an encounter with a loving Savior just cannot keep their joy to themselves. Like the Samaritan woman at the well, Republican women who encounter a loving Savior can persuade the masses and change an entire nation.

CHAPTER 3

RAHAB:
REPUBLICAN WOMEN RECOGNIZE THE PEOPLE AND POWER OF GOD

$\mathcal{T}$he next woman of faith is a prostitute named Rahab (Josh. 2:2). The story of Rahab takes place when Joshua sent two spies to Jericho. These men stayed at what would be considered a brothel today. Nonetheless, the king were apprised of the spies and sent soldiers to the home of Rahab to arrest and kill the spies. Rahab hid the spies, lied to the king's men, and provided a way of passage for the Israeli spies to leave (Josh. 2:4-7).

Before departing, Rahab explained her actions and motives. Rahab, a mere woman—and a prostitute at that—was well aware of the Jews and the success they had in conquering cities and overthrowing kingdoms. She knew that only a god or the true God could part the Red Sea and deliver slaves from Egypt. She knew that their God gave them supernatural favor and success in battle to the point of striking fear in the land. Rahab saved the lives of these men with the hope that they, and their powerful God, would have mercy on her and her entire family when they came to conquer Jericho.

The Word of God says that Rahab petitioned for mercy, saying, "Now then, please swear to me by the Lord that you will show kindness to my family, because I have shown kindness to you. Give me a sure sign that you will spare the lives of my father and mother, my brothers and sisters, and all who belong to them—and that you will save us from death" (Josh. 2:12-13). This seemingly insignificant woman of the night exercised her faith with the hopes of saving her family. She used her shameful circumstance as a prostitute and non-Jew to get the attention of an ever-present God.

Based on the reputation of the Jews, Rahab and her family were going to die. She could have delayed the inevitable by turning these men into the king. She could have curried favor with the king by killing these men herself, in hopes that she and her family would be protected. Instead, Rahab stepped out in faith after recognizing the people of God and understanding the power of God.

As the day draws near to Christ's return, Republican women are shown to be full of faith and understand the times in which they live. Despite overwhelming fear, Republican women push beyond fear and exercise their faith for the sake of their families. The Word of God honors Rahab in the Hall of Faith when it says, "By faith the prostitute Rahab, because she welcomed the spies, was not killed with those who were disobedient" (Heb. 11:31). Like Rahab, Republican women recognize and honor the Almighty God, the people of God, and His Power.

CHAPTER 4

THE NAMELESS PROSTITUTE: REPUBLICAN WOMEN CHOOSE LIFE

This powerful woman is nameless. Not only is she nameless, she is a prostitute with a bastard child. The story concerning this nameless prostitute always focuses on King Solomon; however, the message of this nameless mother is more powerful than the king's wise ruling. The passage in 1 Kings 3 is always used to reveal the wisdom given to Solomon. In fact, even the scriptures describe the "awe" of Solomon's wisdom in devising a rouse to get at the truth of which mother was the rightful mother of the baby. He ordered the baby be split in half, and half was to be given to each woman.

Two women had babies of about the same age and were living in common housing. One woman laid on her child while sleeping and accidentally killed him (1 Kings 3:19). In her grief, she stole the nameless prostitute's baby and replaced it with her dead baby. It goes without saying that every mother knows her child, and the nameless prostitute knew the dead baby was not hers. She then tried to take the baby back from the woman who killed her baby. This child's custody case would prove to be difficult, given that these were mere women—and of low reputation. There was no husband and no father of the child to intervene in the matter. Just two desperate women and the king.

The Word of God reads, "The king said, 'This one says, "My son is alive and your son is dead," while that one says, "No! Your son is dead and mine is alive."' Then the king said, 'Bring me a sword.' So they brought a sword for the king. He then gave an order: 'Cut the living child in two and give half to one and half to the other'" (1 Kings 3:23-25). It came to pass that the real mother, moved only through sincere love for her baby, decided to give the baby away to a scheming, lying, whore abductor, rather than see her baby killed. Indeed, King Solomon ruled wisely, and God's favor was upon him, for God revealed this nameless woman who chose life for her baby to be the "true" mother (I Kings 3:27).

Republican women are on the forefront of the right-to-life movement. These women understand that the most precious gift from God is a child. They distinguish themselves from those who devalue our world's most innocent and precious. It is the passion of Republican women who fearlessly fight to close abortion clinics and defund Planned Parenthood. It is Republican women who will stand, even if alone, on the side of a child's right to be born. Fatherless children, unwanted pregnancies, and babies created from rape and incest deserve Life! Republican women fight for the lives of babies with disabilities whose parents decide to terminate the "imperfection" in the womb. So, it was no coincidence that the Lord allowed this nameless prostitute's story to be told. The determinant of the truth of the "real mother" came from the mother who chose Life! Like the nameless prostitute, Republican women are revealed by the Lord Himself to the wise because Republican women choose Life!

CHAPTER 5

JUDGE DEBORAH:
REPUBLICAN WOMEN JUDGE WISELY

*A*mong the powerful women in the Bible, Prophet and Judge Deborah stands out for her wisdom, courage, and compassionate zeal for justice. There were twelve judges who ruled Israel. Judges four opens with the consistent theme throughout the book, "Again the Israelites did evil in the eyes of the Lord..." (Judg. 4:1). The Word of God reveals the Lord was angry with His children and allowed them to be sold to King Jabin of Canaan. The commander of King Jabin's army was Sisera. Commander Sisera was said to have nine hundred chariots fitted with iron and had cruelly oppressed the Israelites for twenty years (Judg. 4:3). As a result of their dire circumstances, the Israelites cried to the Lord for help.

Deborah was the only woman recorded as the leader of the Israelites (Judg. 4:4). She was a prophet, which means she heard from God, and she was the fourth judge in the line of twelve judges. She was married, and the Bible identifies her as the wife of Lapidoth. Most importantly, Deborah presided over the disputes of Israel. She held court at the Palm of Deborah. After twenty years of oppression, the Lord told Deborah to prepare the men for war against Sisera. The

Lord told her that Sisera would fall at the hands of a woman. Deborah called the Israelites' commander, Barak, to lead the efforts. She told him that not only will the Lord defeat Sisera, but He will do so at the hands of a woman.

As the Lord led Deborah, she accompanied Barak into battle, and the Lord crushed each oppressor. Sisera, the wicked commander, ran on foot to the tent of Jael, the wife of Heber the Kenite. There, Sisera hid and fell asleep. Jael the Kenite took a tent peg and hammer and killed Sisera through the temples. This fulfilled what the Lord had told Prophet and Judge Deborah. When Sisera was found dead, the Israelites were free. The Word of God did not end the story of Deborah there. In fact, Judges 5 recites the song she and Commander Barak sang to the Lord. The song of Deborah and Barak in Judges 5:31 ends with, "So may all your enemies perish, Lord! But may all who love you be like the sun when it rises in its strength." Then the land had peace forty years.

Republican women are leaders, servants of the Lord, wives, mothers, and judges. In the story of Deborah, the Lord selected a woman of virtue and good character to lead His people; this was unheard of in that time. Deborah broke the glass ceiling and then some. She was wise and judicious. She was attuned to God and His voice. She was brave and fearless as she went into battle with Barak. Republican women leaders and jurists possess great virtues and qualities pleasing to God. Like Judge Deborah, Republican women lead without compromising or diminishing their faith, family, and fortitude! Republican women follow the Rule of Law, the only true measure of justice. Republican women take no credit for success; instead, they praise the living God for His deliverance, love, and faithfulness toward His children.

CHAPTER 6

JOCHEBED:
REPUBLICAN WOMEN BUILD ARKS FOR THEIR CHILDREN

One of the most underreported women in the Word of God is Jochebed, mother of Moses. Her name is not mentioned in Exodus 2, which records Moses' birth. Instead, she is in the lineage of Aaron and Moses found in Exodus 6:20: "Amram married his father's sister Jochebed, who bore him Aaron and Moses" What inspired me about Jochebed is that she was not fearful of—nor accepting of—the government's decree that would result in the death of her baby boy. Like Rahab, Jochebed and Amram are listed in the Lord's Hall of Faith. In Hebrews 11:23, the Word of God says, "By faith Moses' parents hid him for three months after he was born, because they saw he was no ordinary child, and they were not afraid of the king's edict."

The Bible says that Jochebed saw that 'he was beautiful' (Ex. 2:3, CSB). Every baby is beautiful, but through the lens of this mother, she recognized something great about her child. Her first inclination was to hide Moses from the destruction of the world. When she could no longer hide him, the Word of God says that Jochebed got a papyrus basket, coated it with tar and pitch, and placed her baby in the Nile (Ex. 2:3). The story continues with Moses' sister Miriam following the baby in the basket down the Nile until the boy is rescued by Pharaoh's daughter. The Lord arranged it so that Moses was nursed by his mother, Jochebed, and adopted into Pharaoh's kingdom.

The Word of God says that Jochebed hid Moses to protect him, and when she could no longer hide him, Jochebed built an ark. The Bible does not say that she placed her son in a basket. I thought it quite odd that her fearless faith in God required more provision and planning, given His plan for the boy. I see the resemblance between Jochebed's ark and Noah's ark. In Noah's ark, the Lord required Noah to build an ark and pitch it with a seal. The destruction of man would not harm Noah and his family in the ark. Likewise, the Lord appeared to do the same for Moses. When the boy was placed in the ark, God also sealed the deliverance of his people.

Jochebed trusted God, and her child became a great leader of his people. Do we see the beauty in our children, or do we look at our babies with disdain and anger? Do we shield our babies as long as we can from a dangerous and ruthless world? What preparations are we making for our children before we have to place them in "the Nile"—or in the world? What future will they have if we allow the world to destroy them? Who is following our children down the river?

Republican women shape the landscape of politics through their children. During a time when children under five were being killed, Jochebed saw beauty and greatness in her child and hid him from danger as long as she could. In a move of great faith and fearlessness, Jochebed made a small ark and trusted God to save her son. Like Jochebed, Republican women see greatness in their children, and they make provisions for their children's lives and futures. Republican women use the "village"—just as Jochebed used Miriam—to protect their children and watch them travel through life. Republican women do not accept death decrees for their babies. Instead, they build arks!

**Sell your books at
sellbackyourBook.com!**
Go to sellbackyourBook.com
and get an instant price quote.
We even pay the shipping - see
what your old books are worth
today!

Inspected By:rosaura

00020874167

0002087 **4167**

CHAPTER 7

HADESSAH:
REPUBLICAN WOMEN ARE PRAYERFUL, FEARLESS ACTIVISTS

*T*he significant woman who shaped the political future of her day was Hadassah, also known as Esther. Hadassah (her Hebrew name) was an orphan raised by her cousin, Mordecai. Mordecai was a central figure in the life of Hadassah and her role in history. According to Strong's Concordance (1998), the name Hadassah means "righteous myrtle tree, a good tree with a pleasing smell.[1]" The prophet Zechariah mentions a vision of a man in between a myrtle tree (Zech. 1:8).

The Book of Esther takes place during the reign of King Xerxes I of Persia. The Persian kings were, for the most part, oppressors of the Jews, and King Xerxes I was not an exception. Hollywood attempted to paint this book and the passages therein as a glamourous love story with a beautiful biblical Cinderella. The truth of Esther and the significance of the Lord allowing her story to be told is one of

---

[1] Strong's Concordance. "Hadassah." BibleHub.com. Accessed June 20, 2018.
http://biblehub.com/hebrew/1919.htm.

lust, oppression, and slavery, threat of death, impalement, annihilation, and the potential genocide of His people.

Mordecai and Hadassah were among those taken captive during the exile by Babylonian King Nebuchadnezzar. There was no true love and romance in this biblical story between the king and the queen. Instead, the Book of Esther focuses on God's amazing love and His powerful hand in delivering His people through a woman willing to die for her people.

King Xerxes loved women—most importantly, beautiful women. He entertained other kings, and on a given occasion he summoned his trophy wife, Queen Vashti. The Word of God indicates Queen Vashti declined to come to the king. This was so disrespectful that the Bible says, "Later when King Xerxes' fury had subsided..." (Esther 2:2); meaning, the king's rage was not short-lived. Queen Vashti was forever banished from the presence of the King. Advisors of the king suggested he look for beautiful virgins in his kingdom to replace Queen Vashti. The king held the first recorded beauty contest in the Bible, and Esther won. The name Esther is derived from the Persian word "star." Esther was so beautiful, the king was attracted to her more than any other woman (Esther 2:17). He considered her his star.

It is believed Hadassah changed her name to Esther to hide her "nationality and family background, because Mordecai had forbidden her to" disclose it (Esther 2:10). The Word of God says that Esther was corralled among the harem of women. She found favor with the lead attendant and was given special food, added maidens for help, and a prime location in the king's harem. Another significant revelation in the story of Esther is that every woman had to prepare for a minimum of one year before they saw the king. The parallelism between Esther's journey and our relationship with our Sovereign God is that we accept and are accepted by King Jesus, but we are not prepared on day one. It takes time and a regimen of cleansing, holiness, and the sweet perfume of the Holy Spirit to be fully prepared for the King of Kings.

This book has been studied in depth, but the actions of Esther are worth revisiting. Esther's cousin and father figure, Mordecai, overheard a plot to assassinate King Xerxes I, and through his report of the plan, his name was given to the king. Mordecai's report of the plot would prove significant to the plan the Lord had in store. In that day, the Jews did not bow to idols nor worship man. Mordecai made an enemy of a favored official of the king's court. This official convinced the king to kill all the Jews. Without question or compassion, King Xerxes I granted the wish of the official and sent a death notice to all of the children of Israel.

In his grief and pain, Mordecai went to the gate of the palace to send word of their fate to the child he raised, Queen Esther. The queen's servant shared with her the request to plead with her husband for the life of the Jewish people. Queen Esther responded with the fear that, since going to the king without being summoned was forbidden, her plea could lead to her death unless he signaled approval. Here is a woman who was married to the man who just issued a decree to mercilessly kill her nation and race of people — a man known to have a hot temper. Mordecai received his daughter's response and told her three things: (1) "Do not think that because you are in the king's house you alone of all the Jews will escape." (2) "For if you remain silent at this time, relief and deliverance for the Jews will arise from another place, but you and your father's family will perish."

(3) "Who knows but that you have come to your royal position for such a time as this?" (Esther 4:13-14).

In response to these powerful words, Queen Esther found courage and told the servant to tell Mordecai to gather all of the Jews. She told them to fast and pray with her, and after three days, she would break the law for her people and go to the king. Finally, this young, beautiful woman told her servant, "And if I perish, I perish" (Esther 4:16b). As it worked out, the Lord used Hadassah to reverse the decree and punish the one who plotted against the Jewish people.

The Hollywood version of the Book of Esther, *One Night with the King* (2006)[2] does not reflect the apathy and wickedness of King Xerxes I nor the power of corporate fasting and praying in the face of severe and imminent threat. Republican women across the nation are faced with situations for which they are not exempt and for which they and their families are in peril. But, "for such a time as this," Republican women have been placed in positions of power and strategic alignment to do the work of the Lord! Republican women understand the power of prayer and fasting and the urgency to address the life and death issues. Like Esther, Republican women are FEARLESS and PRAYERFUL ACTIVISTS set in this world to save a generation of people—including the unborn and uneducated. And, like Esther, if we perish, we perish.

---

[2] *One Night with the King.* Directed by Michael O. Sajbel. Hollywood: Gener8xion Entertainment, 2006.

CHAPTER 8

LOIS AND EUNICE:
REPUBLICAN WOMEN SHARE
THEIR FAITH

*N*ever underestimate the power of a mother and grandmother! Throughout history, the influence of mothers and grandmothers has been evident and remarkable. Notwithstanding a strong father and grandfather in their lives, athletes and actors often attribute their success in their acceptance speech to their mother or grandmother. We also see the impact of mothers and grandmothers in Paul's letters. The Lord allowed the Apostle Paul to craft a second letter of encouragement, direction, instruction, and love to his spiritual son, Timothy. In this second letter, Paul mentions two important women in Timothy's spiritual journey. These are Lois, his grandmother, and Eunice, his mother. This is the only record or mention of these two women in the Bible, but because the Lord makes no mistakes, He thought it worthy of noting.

The second letter from Paul alludes to his imprisonment and suffering on account of the gospel of Jesus. This final letter is poignant and very personal. Paul writes, "Timothy, my dear son: Grace, mercy and peace from God the Father and Christ Jesus our Lord" (2 Tim. 1:2). The urgency of the letter is to remind Timothy to remain firm in the sound teaching of Paul, to not be ashamed of the gospel of Jesus—no matter what the circumstances of the saints—and to be aware of false prophets and teachers. Paul also urges Timothy to come to him in prison and to do so quickly (2 Tim. 4:9).

There is much to learn in the letter from Paul to Timothy. As Christians, we tend to take the seriousness of the letter and the pain that Paul had endured out of context. In the comfort of our plush pulpits and pews, we recite Paul's instructions and words as hymns. This would be Paul's last letter to Timothy, and in this final letter to his beloved son, Paul left nothing of value out.

Paul shares the fact that only Luke the physician remains with him after others had abandoned him in his hour of despair (2 Tim. 4:10-11). At his trial, Paul shares with Timothy that not a single person came to his defense except for the Lord Himself (2 Tim. 4:16-18). Only then did he escape what would be his fate in the mouths of the lions (2 Tim. 4:17b). The pain of Paul's letter also mentions and warns Timothy of the extreme harm that Paul experienced from Alexander the metal worker (2 Tim. 4:14).

In the midst of the warnings against false teachers and doctrines and the encouragement to stand firm in sound teaching without fear when faced with persecution, the Lord, through Paul, provides another glimpse of the important role of Lois and Eunice in the life of Timothy. Paul writes, "But as for you, continue in what you have learned and have become convinced of, because you know those from whom you learned it, and how from infancy you have known the Holy Scriptures, which are able to make you wise for salvation through faith in Christ Jesus (2 Tim. 3:14-15).

From infancy, Timothy learned the holy scriptures, which were able to make him wise for salvation through faith in Christ Jesus. This powerful affirmation of the work of his grandmother Lois and his mother Eunice clearly demonstrates how these women shared their faith with Timothy. When he was a child, they taught him the Word of God, and it changed the world. It is clear these women modeled Christ in front of both Timothy and those they encountered.

Lois and Eunice are two women who left an everlasting legacy and were intentionally recorded in the pages of the Bible. Like Timothy's grandmother and mother, Republican women unashamedly share their sincere faith in God. These mothers and grandmothers instill the Word of God and truth to their children and grandchildren from infancy. Republican women know the power of God's Word to save, sustain, restore, remind, and resurrect. In sharing their faith, Republican mothers and grandmothers honor the Lord and are raising up an army to build the kingdom of God on this earth.

CHAPTER 9

MARY, MOTHER OF JESUS: REPUBLICAN WOMEN ARE EFFECTIVE LOBBYISTS

*W*ithout a doubt, the most famous woman recorded in the Bible is Mary, the mother of Jesus. She is revered, dearly loved, and treasured. In several Christian segments, Mary is a saint. Still, what the twenty-first century person thinks of this imperfect yet chosen and amazing woman of God is irrelevant. The Lord Himself told Mary through an angel that she was "highly favored," that He "was with her," and that she was "blessed among women" (Lk. 1:28). The Bible says that this greeting troubled and confused her. Mary was obviously very humble, pure in heart, overwhelmed, and yet, not self-seeking. This young girl would be the mother of the Sovereign God. She had no idea what was going to occur in her life or that of her baby.

The record of Mary and her background has been taught and televised for all mankind. To delve into her lineage, background, and persona would consume millions of pages. The chaos, scandal, and drama concerning her surprise pregnancy required the Lord to intervene with her betrothed, Joseph. To add to the stress of life, this poor young and pregnant woman would not be able to deliver the baby inside of a home or an inn. Rather, she gave birth to Jesus in a filthy pen for animals and laid the Savior in a random food trough, or a manger.

The same night of Jesus' birth, shepherds visited Joseph and Mary in the manger and began to proclaim Jesus as the Messiah. The celebration and worship of Mary's baby boy must have been remarkable. The Word of God says, "But Mary treasured up all these things and pondered them in her heart" (Lk. 2:19). As required by Jewish law, Jesus was circumcised on the eighth day, and sometime later, He was taken to Jerusalem to be purified, as was custom. Joseph and Mary encountered a righteous and devout man named Simeon who, under the Holy Spirit of God, affirmed to the parents that Jesus was the Messiah and Savior of the world. The Bible says, "The child's father and mother marveled at what was said about him" (Lk. 2:33). Soon after, Joseph and Mary returned with Jesus to Galilee to the town of Nazareth.

When Jesus was twelve years old, His parents took Him to Jerusalem for the Festival of the Passover. When Passover ended, Joseph and Mary began their journey home and had traveled for more than a day when they realized their son Jesus was not among them. Three days later, they found Jesus with the teachers at the temple, who were listening, asking, and answering questions. All who encountered Him marveled. As any mother would, Mary chided Him for being absent, but Jesus reminded her that He had to be about His Father's business. While Joseph and Mary did not understand what Jesus was saying at the time, Jesus left with His parents, and the Bible says that He "was obedient to them" (Lk. 2:51) Again, the Word of God says, "But his mother treasured all these things in her heart" (Lk. 2:51).

This woman who helped fulfill the plan of God was the mother of the Messiah. While she is known to most of us, there is one instance of her leadership worth sharing. At the time when Jesus was beginning His ministry, He had been rejected in Nazareth, baptized, and tested in the wilderness, and He called His disciples. Mary, the mother of Jesus, was invited to a wedding banquet in Cana of Galilee, as was Jesus and His disciples. As it was custom, the banquet host would serve the best and finest wine first while leaving the cheaper wine for last. The wedding host ran into a dilemma, in that the guests completely ran out of wine!

The Gospel of John records what took place at this wedding banquet and highlights Mary's significance to God. When the wine was gone, Jesus' mother said to him, "They have no more wine"(Jn. 2:3). Jesus—the Messiah, Son of Man, Son of God, Savior of the World, King of kings and Lord of lords—told Mary in so many words that the wine was not His business and that His time had not yet come (Jn. 2:4). Mary—the mother of Jesus, the woman who experienced, saw, and heard the Word of God about her son—knew that He could fix this problem. Mary also remembered all the things she kept in her heart concerning her son Jesus. Ignoring her son's remarks, Mary gathered the servants in the banquet to follow Jesus' instructions, whatever they would be. Jesus turned the water into wine, the bridegroom was hailed for serving "choice wine," and all was well.

The Bible does not say that Jesus had performed any miracles up to this point. In fact, it is widely accepted among theologians and Christian leaders that this was Jesus' first miracle. This story also shows Mary as an effective lobbyist. Mary wielded her authority and position to meet the need of this family at the wedding, and she knew her son was the source for which this miracle could happen. Despite her son's desire to stay out of the trivial affairs of a wedding banquet, Mary said only a few words to the nearby servants: "Do whatever he tells you" (Jn. 2:5).

Mary's request reflects her understanding of her son's authority, as well as her influence. Jesus would go on to heal lepers, open blinded eyes, cast out demons, feed multitudes, raise people from the dead, and more. Yet, turning water into wine was His first miracle. Why? Because He had been shown to be obedient and respectful to His mother. And, His mother asked Him to do this miracle. Like Mary, the mother of Jesus, Republican women understand power, influence, and how to petition and lobby those in authority. Republican women use personal relationships to advance a worthy cause. We honor Mary's eternal role in history and her example as a leader among women.

CHAPTER 10

JOANNA AND SUZANNA: REPUBLICAN WOMEN ARE GENEROUS DONORS

*T*wo women who shaped the political future of their day were Joanna and Susanna. These two women are only mentioned briefly in Luke 8:3 and were selected because the Word of God says that they provided financial support to Jesus and His twelve disciples. To understand the motivation behind Joanna and Susanna, it is important to know the context in which the Lord inserts them into the pages of history.

In the last part of Luke 7, Jesus is anointed by what the Bible calls a "sinful" woman (Lk. 7:37). This woman heard about the arrival of Jesus at the home of a Pharisee and took an alabaster jar of perfume. The sinful woman fell down, crying and kissing the Savior's feet. She then anointed His feet and wiped them with her hair. The gospel describes the encounter as offensive to the Pharisee, who suggested that Jesus is no prophet if He doesn't know what type of woman is touching Him. Just then, Jesus told Simon the leper a parable about a debtor who owes much and a debtor who owes little (Mk. 14:3). Jesus asked which debtor would be more grateful. Simon replied that it would be the one to whom much was forgiven. Jesus affirmed his answer and rebuked the Pharisee. The Lord then told the woman that she was forgiven and that her faith had saved her.

Luke, the writer of the gospel under the unction of the Holy Spirit, inserted many women into his writings. The nameless sinful woman was forgiven as she demonstrated her love for Christ through the gesture of giving Him what Mark called a very expensive jar of perfume (Mk. 14:3), which was worth a year's salary (Mk. 14:5). No doubt this gesture was out of sincere love and gratitude for Jesus.

Likewise, Luke opens Chapter 8 with a glimpse of the people—both men and women—who were following Jesus. The Word of God says that Jesus and His disciples traveled "and also some women who had been cured of evil spirits and diseases: Mary (called Magdalene) from whom seven demons had come out; Joanna the wife of Chuza, the manager of Herod's household; Susanna; and many others. These women were helping to support them out of their own means" (Lk. 8:2-3). The Bible does not say how Jesus delivered these women, but the Word of God clearly recognizes the role women played in promoting and funding the ministry of Jesus.

The campaign for the kingdom of God began with twelve disciples but was fully supported by women. Major donors are essential in delivering a message, and this was the case for Jesus and the twelve. Jesus could have turned garbage into gold or rocks into rubies to finance His ministry, but His purpose was not wealth and riches; it was the heart of man. Jesus was preparing the world for the kingdom and the citizens in that kingdom. He spoke of cheerful giving, sacrificial giving, and giving out of love rather than compulsion. Joanna and Susanna were grateful women who had been delivered or healed by Jesus in some way, and they provided for the gospel out of their own means.

Joanna and Susanna invested in eternity. Like Joanna and Susanna, Republican women support and invest their own money into a cause in which they believe. Every great and worthy cause on this earth has required financial support. Political activism can also be financial. Giving to advance the political conservative message and momentum is very important. Republican women are grateful to God for His love toward us through the death and resurrection of His Son Jesus. Republican women give generously to those causes and charities that promote the kingdom and the values expressed by our Savior. Conservative women are good stewards, and they can shape the future of politics through their generosity.

CHAPTER 11

MARY, MOTHER OF JOHN MARK: REPUBLICAN WOMEN PRAY

*T*his brief and honorable mention of Mary, mother of John Mark, in Acts 12 was another testament to both the love God has for women and the power of prayer. Conceivably, all Christians at the time were to be put to death, and as a result, many had scattered. The author of the Book of Acts, Luke the physician, wrote two letters to Theophilus. These are the Gospel of Luke and the Book of Acts. Luke shares that he "carefully investigated everything from the beginning... to write an orderly account... so that he may know the certainty of the things he has been taught" (Lk 1:3-4). Women are interwoven through the copious writings of Dr. Luke, and he mentioned this woman, Mary, mother of John—also called Mark—for a reason.

The passage in Acts 12 speaks of Peter's miraculous escape from prison. The disciple James, brother of John, was put to death by sword. This was a significant blow to the followers of Jesus. After noticing that this pleased some of the Jews, King Herod was very confident that killing all Christ-followers would be welcomed by the Jews. Herod then arrested Peter. The Word of God reveals, "but the church was earnestly praying to God for him" (Acts 12:5).

This is significant. Of those identified as the "church," it was very clear that women were part of this important and faithful act: prayer.

Peter was released from prison and went to the home of Mary, mother of John—also called Mark—right away. A servant named Rhoda met him at the door, and she was so overwhelmed by the answered prayer that she shut the door on him. She then proclaimed, "Peter is at the door!" but they thought she had lost her mind or that Peter was an angel (Acts 12:14-15). When they finally opened the door, Peter asked Mary and the others to share with James and the other brothers what the Lord did.

Mary, mother of John Mark, was likely dealing with the tragic and devastating deaths of the disciples. Peter was arrested just after the disciple James was killed. While others fled and some denounced the faith, this woman convened a group to pray for Peter. Not much is said about the communication between Peter and the followers of the Way, but the Bible clearly states that Peter was guarded by sixteen soldiers (Acts 12:4). In fact, Peter found himself chained between two guards. The Fort Knox of security was not enough for our God! This woman named Mary and others were praying to an attentive and loving Father who, without a doubt, inclined His ear to their cries and prayers. In response, the Lord set Peter free.

Luke begins the Book of Acts with a description of praying women. Luke writes of the time that Jesus spent with His disciples as He shared with them that they must remain in Jerusalem to receive the gift that God had promised (Acts 1:4). The Word of God says the eleven apostles (as Judas Iscariot hung himself on a tree) returned to Jerusalem to wait on the gift. Luke continues to write, "They all joined together constantly in prayer, along with the women and Mary the mother of Jesus, and with his brothers" (Acts 1:14). No matter the era or century, from the beginning of time, women were, are, and will always be very important to God.

Like Mary, mother of John Mark, Republican women pray. In fact, Republican women toss caution aside — political correctness be damned — and unashamedly pray. Each year during the National Day of Prayer, Republican women are fasting, praying, and interceding for our government, nation, and leaders (1 Tim. 2:1-4). Each Saturday for some and Sunday for others, Republican women join with other believers and followers of Christ to pray earnestly for their families, communities, and friends (Heb. 10:25). Every day and every moment of the day, a Republican woman is praying (Eph. 6:18). Our nation, with all of its flaws is sustained by the prayers of praying women (James 5:16)!

CHAPTER 12

JEPHTHAH'S DAUGHTER:
REPUBLICAN WOMEN ARE COMMITTED TO THE END

*T*he daughter of Jephthah is a powerful story of faithfulness, commitment, and love for God. Jephthah was a mighty warrior. He was the son of Gilead, and his mother was a prostitute with whom Gilead committed adultery (Judg. 11:1). Jephthah was a descendent of Joseph through Manasseh, Makir, and his father, Gilead (Num. 26:28-29). This fine lineage would make any man proud, but it was short-lived. Gilead's wife had sons, and when they got older, they banned their father's bastard son from the clan. Jephthah left and led a band of scoundrels in the land of Tob (Judg. 11:2-3).

Israel was being threatened by the king of the Ammonites, and representatives went to Tob to seek out their mightiest warrior, Jephthah. Jephthah questioned their motives and sincerity but went home with them to take command of their army. Jephthah received a letter from the king of the Ammonites to surrender the land, and he replied with his own letter, which stated that the land was given by God and that only He would judge who gets it (Judg. 11:4-28).

The Word of God says that the Spirit of the Lord came upon Jephthah, and his success in battle was only by the hands of God. In his gratitude to God, Jephthah made a vow to the Lord, saying, "If you give the Ammonites into my hands, whatever comes out of the door of my house to meet me when I return in triumph from the Ammonites will be the Lord's, and I will sacrifice it as a burnt offering" (Judg. 11:30-31). This vow to God is the reason for honoring Jephthah's daughter.

The Lord delivered the Ammonites into Jephthah's hands, and he was celebrated over the land. When Jephthah returned home, instead of an animal coming out of his door, Jephthah's young daughter came out, dancing and singing. This young girl—his only child—had no idea that her father made a vow to God. She had no idea that her life would forever change. Jephthah wept bitterly and told his daughter that he made an unbreakable vow (Judg. 11:32-34).

The young girl responded in a way that would be difficult, if not impossible for a young person today. She said, "You have given your word to the Lord. Do to me just as you promised, now that the Lord has avenged you of your enemies, the Ammonites. But grant me this one request," she said. "Give me two months to roam the hills and weep with my friends, because I will never marry" (Judg.11:36-37). This profound response is worthy of honor and respect. This young girl put her father, her people, and her future before her own life. She requested time to grieve, but a vow made to God was more important than her life.

It is difficult to know how many women would die for a vow made to the Lord. The girl must have shared in the shame of being banished from her people when they moved to Tob. She must have seen the pain in her father as he was leading nothing more than a gang of thugs. Jephthah's daughter must have been proud when the elders sought her father's help to defeat their enemy. She must have seen her father restored and promoted to commander of the army. So, when faced with honoring God or disgracing her family by breaking the vow, this young woman accepted her fate with grace, compassion, pride, and love.

Jephthah's daughter had only one request. She desired to go away to be with her friends. When she returned, she was sacrificed, as Jephthah promised God. The Bible says, "From this comes the Israelite tradition that each year the young women of Israel go out for four days to commemorate the daughter of Jephthah the Gileadite" (Judg. 11:39b-40).

What can Republican women learn from Jephthah's nameless daughter? We can learn that our vows matter. They matter to God, to our spouses, to our children, and to our community. We can learn that some of our sisters are dealing with terminal life circumstances, and like the friends of Jephthah's daughter, we need to be there for them until the end. Finally, Republican women can learn that commitment to the end is needed in all aspects of our lives. God will get the glory for our obedience and sacrifice.

FROM DYED TO DIED IN THE WOOL

REPUBLICAN WOMEN
EMULATE CHRIST

*T*his book provides a glimpse of the amazing qualities, character, and attributes of a select few women in the Word of God. As such, it is my prayer that every woman, especially Republican women reflect on the life and contribution of (1) Zelophehad's five daughters, (2) the Samaritan woman, (3) Rahab, (4) The Nameless Prostitute, (5) Judge Deborah, (6) Jochebed, (7) Hadessah, (8) Lois and Eunice, (9) Mary, Mother of Jesus, (10) Joanna and Suzanna, (11) Mary, Mother of John Mark, and (12) Jephthah's Daughter. Individually, these wonderful and blessed women shine. Collectively, their passion, humility, kindness, resolve, faith, determination, submission, fearlessness, and love are found in only one: Christ Jesus.

I met the Lord Jesus many years ago in Lansing, Michigan. He was and remains a very real and present help and my loving Lord and Savior. As a Christian, I am unapologetic about my desire to please God and represent, glorify, and emulate Him on this earth. The Word of God refers to Jesus as the Lamb of God (Jn. 1:29), as well as the Lamb that was slain (Rev. 3:8). The Bible gives few descriptions of Jesus' physical appearance, but His second coming describes our Lamb as having hair as white as wool. It is this precious Lamb who died that I may live. I too, must die with Christ, the Lamb, so that His work and witness may draw others (Rom. 6:7-9). Thus, I am no longer "dyed in the Wool," as so eloquently stated by Frederick Douglass, rather, I am now *died* in the Wool of my Savior, Christ Jesus.

Endnotes

1. BrainyQuote. "Frederick Douglass Quotes."
    BrainyQuote.com (201568). Accessed June
    20, 2018. https://www.brainyquote.com/quotes/
    frederick_douglass_201568.

2. BrainyQuote. "Frederick Douglass Quotes."
    BrainyQuote.com (201568). Accessed June
    20, 2018. https://www.brainyquote.com/quotes/
    frederick_douglass_201568.

NOTES

BrainyQuote. "Frederick Douglass Quotes." BrainyQuote. com (201568). Accessed June 20, 2018. https://www. brainyquote.com/quotes/frederick_douglass_201568

One Night with the King. Directed by Michael O. Sajbel. Hollywood: Gener8xion Entertainment, 2006.

9 781545 639672